in books a...
was the birth...
revolution. 'Quality...
a packet of cigarettes, ...
for the first time, a nation of ...
nation of book-buyers – and the ...
publishing was changed for ever, ...
principles – of quality and value, with an ...
belief in the fundamental importance of reading ...
have guided everything the company has ...
done since 1935. Sir Allen Lane's ...
pioneering spirit is still very much alive ...
at Penguin in 2005. Here's to ...
the next 70 years!

MORE THA...

'We decided it was time to end the almost ...
hearted manner in which cheap editions were p...
though the only people who could possibly want cheap...
must belong to a lower order of intelligence. We, howev...
believed in the existence in this country of a vast reading publi...
for intelligent books at a low price, and staked everything on it'
Sir Allen Lane, 1902–1970

'The Penguin Books are splendid value for sixpence, so
splendid that if other publishers had any sense they would
combine against them and suppress them'
George Orwell

'More than a business … a national cultural asset'
Guardian

'When you look at the whole Penguin achievement you know
that it constitutes, in action, one of the more democratic
successes of our recent social history'
Richard Hoggart

Under the Clock

New Poems by
TONY HARRISON

PENGUIN BOOKS

PENGUIN BOOKS

Published by the Penguin Group
Penguin Books Ltd, 80 Strand, London WC2R ORL, England
Penguin Group (USA) Inc., 375 Hudson Street, New York, New York 10014, USA
Penguin Group (Canada), 10 Alcorn Avenue, Toronto, Ontario, Canada M4V 3B2
(a division of Pearson Penguin Canada Inc.)
Penguin Ireland, 25 St Stephen's Green, Dublin 2, Ireland
(a division of Penguin Books Ltd)
Penguin Group (Australia), 250 Camberwell Road, Camberwell, Victoria 3124,
Australia (a division of Pearson Australia Group Pty Ltd)
Penguin Books India Pvt Ltd, 11 Community Centre,
Panchsheel Park, New Delhi – 110 017, India
Penguin Group (NZ), cnr Airborne and Rosedale Roads, Albany,
Auckland 1310, New Zealand (a division of Pearson New Zealand Ltd)
Penguin Books (South Africa) (Pty) Ltd, 24 Sturdee Avenue,
Rosebank 2196, South Africa

Penguin Books Ltd, Registered Offices: 80 Strand, London WC2R ORL, England

www.penguin.com

First published as a Pocket Penguin 2005

1

Copyright © Tony Harrison, 2005
All rights reserved

The moral right of the author has been asserted

14306

ACKNOWLEDGEMENTS
Some of these poems first appeared in
Arion (Boston, USA)
The *Guardian*
In Coda Per Caronte (Einaudi)
The *Independent on Sunday*
London Review of Books
Marxist Quarterly
Stand

Set in 11/13pt Monotype Dante
Typeset by Palimpsest Book Production Limited
Polmont, Stirlingshire
Printed in England by Clays Ltd, St Ives plc

Contents

The Krieg Anthology

I

THE HEARTS AND MINDS OPERATION

'Decapitation' to win minds and hearts,
a bombing bruited surgical, humane, 's
only partially successful when its start 's
a small child's shrapnelled scalp scooped
   of its brains.

II

MIRROR IMAGE

Forced indoors with shining sun outside,
a child of seven who should have peace to play
on a swing, a roundabout, a slide
slid out on a chilled morgue metal tray.

III

COMFORTER

Maybe she was teething up to her last day!
The dummy with smeared honey on its tip 's
to soothe the fretful babe till USA
grab life and plastic nipple from her lips.

IV
RICE PADDY

'US Airborne 's not there to escort
kids to school,' snorts Condoleeza.
'No, not to school,' I counter-snort,
'but to the mortuary freezer.'

V
THE BODY RE-COUNT

Dead Iraqis vote BUSH after all!
Florida's Bushibboleth 's become Baghdad's.
He's re-elected by them as they fall
with flayed-off human flesh like hanging chads.

VI
ROSE PARADE

Sorry they're shrivelled, your liberators' petals!
There's no water here to keep the flowers fresh
though your laser-guided shower of shattering metal 's
sown these damp red roses in our flesh.

VII
SHAKE, PARDNER!

Bush, who dragged him into this mad folly
though shown flag and painted V and
   warning flare,

will, like the A10 'cowboy on a jolly',
with friendly fire, finish Tony Blair.

VIII
FAVOURS

The friendly fire from George Bush and his pards
rains on Tony Blair who shrieks *et tu!*,
like so many open wounds from bomblet shards
spattered party rosettes, blue on blue.

IX
BAGHDAD LULLABY

Ssshhh! Ssshhh! though now shrapnel makes
    you shriek
and deformities in future may brand you as
    a freak,
you'll see, one day, disablement 's a blessing
    and a boon
sent in baby-seeking bomblets by benefactor
    Hoon.

X
ILLINOIS ELEGY

My son's remains come back for me to grieve.
They'd've brought me more to bury if they could.
They went to so much trouble to retrieve
the DNA smear on this cotton bud.

HOLY TONY'S PRAYER

Why is it, Lord, although I'm right
I find it hard to sleep at night?
Sometimes I wake up in a sweat
they've not found WMDs yet!
The thought that preys most on my mind,
is the only arms they'll ever find
(unless somehow I get MI6
to plant them to be found by Blix,
that's *if* the UN sneaks back in)
are Ali's in the surgeon's bin.
Ali Ismail Abbas who
is a sick Iraqi PR coup.

Lord, Thou must divinely care
for Thy servant Tony Blair
since Thou decreed I was created
morally more elevated
and by Thy grace created blessed
with clearer conscience than the rest.
When little children squeal in pain
my conscience, Lord, 's without a stain.
Thou knowest that my conscience, Lord,
for all the bloodflow stays unflawed.
I unleash terror without taint
a sort of (dare one say it?) saint!
Miraculous! No moral mire
soils my immaculate attire.

None of the blood and shit of war
ever clogs a single pore.
What a good boy am I, Jack Horner
self-cleansing in his moral sauna.
At Camp David dinner I say Grace
with my most holy parson's face.
Though brother George requires no prod
to bring your name up often, God,
fact is I competed with my host
to see who can mention Thee the most.
Lord, buff now my halo's sheen
dimmed now that the nation 's seen
Ali Ismail Abbas who
is a sick Iraqi PR coup,
the bandaged forehead to enhance
the pathos of his helpless glance.
Poor Cherie's throat gets a small lump
when Ali waves his bandaged stump.
It made me think, Lord, that they'd win
if we can't contrive some counterspin
against this winsome amputee
specially created for TV.
They held a country-wide audition
to undermine the coalition.
Let 's hint that vile Iraqi guile
chooses a boy with eyes and smile
that melt the heart, then (how I hate
such callous brutes!) amputate
both his arms with blunt axe hack.
The British 'll buy that from Iraq!

5

I need a spokesman, Hoon for choice,
he 's got the gall and boring voice,
someone like Geoff Hoon to say
how Ali's mother will one day
(oops, can't, sorry I forgot
our bomb, apart from Ali, killed the lot)
mothers 'll draw comfort from
the coalition cluster bomb.
Then once hostilities soon stop
there'll be a brilliant photo op
outside with me at number 10
(yes, I'll still be PM then!)
outside number 10 with me,
once every Saddam statue 's downed,
Ali with prosthetic V!
(Twist his wrist the right way round.)

XII

EPILOGUE to *THE RECRUITING OFFICER*
of Mr FARQUHAR
spoken by MR REDGRAVE from the stage of the
Garrick Theatre, Lichfield, September 2003

You might consider me more brazen if I doff
my feathered hat, and bluff persona off,
and as my brazen self stand up and say
what else our Farquhar might put in his play.
I tell you that our playwright Mr Farquhar
could have made your evening a lot darker
and made our play uncomfortably black

by showing you recruiting for Iraq,
and war management in Tony Blair's UK,
the doctored facts, the dodgy dossier,
that sent deluded soldiers overseas
on the strength of spurious WMDs.
Suckers fell for our recruiters' tricks
and took the shilling in 1706,
now they are conned, the suckers of our times,
when Brazen Blair doles out George Bush's dimes.
Seek recruiters in our cast you won't find any,
not Neve, Harry, Brendan, Harley, Petra, Penny,
and the recruiter's job is absolutely foreign
to Owen and to James, and to me, Corin.
As Kite and Plume and Brazen we'd dragoon
the deluded and the duped for Mr Hoon,
but as ourselves we'd damn Hoon, Blair and Straw
and drum up people to condemn their war.
We're resisters not recruiters, anti- not pro-wars.
Pray show which you prefer by your applause.
Hats on, recruiters!

                Off, resisters!

                       Pro-?

                            Or anti-wars?
Pray show which you prefer by your applause!

XIII

OFF THE SCENT

Thank God (the PM's pal) he's not resigned
and still here to lead his party from behind.

Though not actually voting he was there
in spirit to spare the fox, our caring Blair
whose far far shriller view halloos
set off packs of Tomahawks and Cruise,
Blair in his Iraq-hued hunting coat,
whose cheeks with Bush-brush daubings bloat
when he blows hard on Herod's hunting horn
to cluster-bomb the cradle-culled newborn,
whose taste for dismemberment 's more amputees
hunted by helicopters and Humvees.

Species Barrier

An Afghan mega food-aid drop
this plump cow banquet, but no parachute,
not carved up into packs of steak and chop,
or some collaterally slaughtered brute?

Or is it a whole cow colony of spores
with no rushed R & D to 'weaponize',
an FMD carcass with raw sores,
the staggers stampeding from the skies?

Not aid-drop mega-feast, not germ warfare
though it's pregnant with explosive, putrid gas,
this maggot Mecca crescendoing with prayer
will never feed the hungry folk who pass.

An Afghan's total herd like some gunned stray
from culled Cumbria dumped on Kabul,
the colluding cabinet of the hooked UK
still committing its 'contiguous cull'.

The Ode Not Taken

C. T. Thackrah (1799–1833)

Dissecting corpses with Keats at Guy's,
Leeds-born Thackrah shared the poet's TB.
Cadavers that made Keats poeticize
made Thackrah scorn the call of poetry.

Praising the Classics to the *Lit. & Phil.*,
versed in Greek and Latin, and Eng. Lit.,
he scribbled no sonnets on the scribbling mill
but penned descriptions of the scribblers' shit.
Could write hexameters by Virgil's rules,
and parrot Latin epics but he chose
flax-hecklers' fluxes with their 'gruelly' stools,
the shit of Yorkshire operatives, in prose.

But there are pentameters in Thackrah's tract,
the found iambics no prose can destroy,
which want to stop the heart with simple fact:

we do not find old men in this employ.

Under the Clock

Under Dyson's clock in Lower Briggate
was where my courting parents used to meet.
It had a Father Time and *Tempus Fugit*
sticking out sideways into the street
above barred windows full of wedding bands,
'eternities' to be inscribed with names,
like that I felt on dad's when we held hands,
or on mam's crumbling finger in cremation's
    flames.

Today back on Briggate I stopped and saw
the red hands on the Roman XII and V
those lovers won't meet under any more,
glad stooping Father Time and I survive.
I see the scythe, the hourglass, the wings,
the Latin you'd proudly ask me to construe
and think of the padded boxes with your rings,
under the clock to keep our rendezvous.

Gaps

Sitting in the ferry's stern, my son, my Dad,
with a gap where I'd been till I took these snaps.
Both wear fur hats I'd brought from Leningrad
in Cold War days before the Wall's collapse.

Dad's, though his mates mocked, got lots of wear.
On his Leeds United terrace his bald head
was kept snug by Siberian brown bear.
My daughter 's got his hat, but Dad 's long dead.

My son's was made of rabbit and he gnawed
the fur off it in clumps when we saw *Jaws*.
He didn't need it in the locked hot ward,
his visions frightening as the First Gulf War's.

This snap 's a snatched but happy family scene,
bright New York winter sun between two showers
shining on both of them, and in between
the World Trade Center's unbombarded towers.

Amazon

At the watery border
of three countries,
(one eliminated early,
two still in the running,)
tethered to thick trees
the floating house
with foundations of gators
strains on its moorings
so the satellite rocks
and the football flickers.

Swinging in hammocks
watching the World Cup
on dodgy reception
with six macaws
feathered in fan strip,
blue, yellow, red,
Colombia's colours,
swigging shots of cane-hooch
men shout at the screen,
when Colombia scores,
and *gol! gol! gol!*
yell the loyal macaws.

Outside on the verandah
the world's biggest rat
the pig-size *chiguero* 's
almost wholly devoured
the national team calendar,
and a black boy in blonde wig,
El Pibe Valderrama's curls,
balanced on felled floating timber
on currents full of piranhas
boots his World Cup ball
from his log to his sister's
who gets her own yellow wig
under her brilliant header
of the, till then dry, ball into the flood
of the Amazon where it swirls
and bobs from Colombia to Peru
past pink dolphins and sawmill
through rubber trees on to Brazil
and the downstream fish-market
where a black-scaled fish just sliced
in six still writhing slices
bloods the white marble and a priest
makes grunting gourmet noises
under a glass Parisian roof
where non-fan flocks of parrots,
untrained for the touchline,
fly like a curtain over the glazing,
team jerseys shredded to pixels
showering from shouted-at screens,
a cloudburst of dazzle and hue
over Colombia, Brazil, Peru.

The Gifts of Aphrodite

These figs missed the picker
moved to pluck tokens
of love or welcome to strangers,
missed bird, missed casual snacker,
so are burst and outspread
as red as hibiscus,
scuffed pistil opera plush,
carmine mite-view velveteen
the pile of posh bath robes.

The carob pods clatter,
as the woman rattles
her long pole in the tree,
down through the branches
to the roadside ditch
from which she picks a handful
as we pass her: *'Take, sweet
as honey. Eat! Eat!'*
All Eve's kin and as kind
with their sweet temptations
nuts, ripe figs, pears,
a fragrant herb to smell,
thyme, basil, oregano . . .

a red pomegranate flower
a sprig of white jasmine.

Then as we walked, hot and thirsty,
a groaning green truck
laden with leafy oranges
driven by a black-clad priest
drove past us. 'Catch!' he cried.
The flung rogue orange
rolled down the dusty hill
till stopped by a wicket
of three roadside asphodels
that went on gently vibrating
the chord of thankful receivers.
I held the fruit high
in greeting and gratitude
at the retreating truck,
a sunburst reflected
then eclipsed in the cassock.

At the Baths of Aphrodite
where bathing 's forbidden
a first fig leaf falls
yellowing into the pool
with shed off-white dove fluff
startling the basking eel
suppler than asphodels
into two brief shudders
from an I to an S
and back, twice:

IS it spells IS
the be all and end all
settling to a still I.

At dawn we swim the sun up
over blue/purple mountains
as the swordfish flotilla
heads back to harbour and docks,
tonight's feast aboard
in fresh bloody slices.

11 *September* 2001

For Alfie in Cyprus

Turquoise, indigo, the water
I teach my grandson to love,
who now chews his octopus
swirled in oil and oregano
an inch of tentacle gnawed
and another, savouring the strange,
oil dribbles over his belly,
laughing at everything
was at birth not even a kilo,
so premature he only just made it,
and whose little heart racing
I saw slow down the first time
out of his tent in his mother's arms
the monitor's red digits decreasing,
so he needs no lessons in loving the life
he scarcely scraped into,
but today I made a wish
that all the gifts of this morning,
clear comforting water
so joyfully splashed in,
his octopus, *Sprite*,
pomegranate in yoghurt,
at a beach not that far from

British Army manoeuvres,
and wild forest and mountains,
in an island divided
by bankrupt religions
both bred in the desert,
is all Alfie will ever crave
of Paradise.

Florida Frost

Cancer carried off his cherished wife
as Florida floundered in a freak harsh freeze
and let the Fahrenheit out of his life
never to gain back its lost degrees.
He still can't quite believe she's wholly lost.
He no more thought he'd see his dear one go
than that he'd see in Florida a frost
with that sudden drop last year to 12 below.

Grapefruit froze then splurted slush.
Unripe oranges were cold and hard.
Tears were shed for many a blighted bush
in every northern Florida backyard.
Pipless tangelos with loose zipper skins
flashed frozen segments with a sound like
    farts.
Burst pith with ice spikes like a hexer's pins
hammered in to atrophy those parts.

Literally glacé, ice-candied rind
rims the ruined kumquats with a shine,
moonshafts from shadows, they're the kind
served by Pluto to sad Proserpine.

Stacks of citrus branches burned all night
and glowed through the window of his
   sharpening shed
onto rows of glittering teeth that soon would bite
into more local orchards that were dead.

A man brought in his grandad's old two-hander –
felling an orchard was a chore to share,
a source of grief to grower goose and gander
so he asks his wife to go Dutch on despair.
Her grip on the other handle steels his nerves.
She hears, as the kumquat crown bows to the blade,
the boiling pock-pock of a life's preserves
then collapsing pantry shelves of marmalade.

He gets a different memory from the saw,
and feels the rhythms they once used in love,
though the bedsprings aren't so squeaky any more,
in the old two-hander that they pull and shove.
Gratified greed gives saws their grin.
Whether a moist juice dribbles down its jaw
or just a few dry crumbs stick to its chin,
any wood seems toothsome to a saw.

The moist eyes move from new cut stump to stump
of trees that never failed them, and just last year
fruited when she found her frightening lump
and the whole house reeked with jamming
   and joint fear.
Now he sharpens saws with relish for them both,

bitter that the bright oncologist maligned
their glorious groves by calling cancer 'growth'
and all day the whetted teeth have whined and
    dined.

Never had saws more venom in their bite.
Never did fruit trees struggle less to fall.
Why shouldn't Florida feel freezing blight
walk in from the groves and touch them all?
One Sunday his sense of loss sent him berserk –
another turkeyless repast to face alone.
He took the mower out and made short work
of everything his wife had ever grown.

Earth dragged down his darling and his dear
and considered it just recompense to toss
hydrangeas his direction once a year.
All Busch Gardens weren't worth such a loss.
What happened to vast acres north and west
of central Florida attacked his wife;
the icy Celsius gnawed at her breast
and robbed the Citrus State of half its life.

Cremation Eclogue

Pig pyres are crackling in the snow-flecked fields,
dawn bonfires next to cleaned-out byres and
    folds.
I know my taxi driver. FMD,
the tragic traincrash (ten dead) yesterday
are what we talk about: Heddon-on-the-Wall
may be infected from untreated swill,
the micro virus and the cattle plague
that could cross borders between bloc and bloc
when the world was so divided, let alone
unpatrolled farm fences, ditch and lane.
The taxi's heater's fierce, we discuss
the icicles hanging from the underpass,
this zero morning as we track the Tyne
and follow the Station signposts towards town.

I was in what was then Leningrad
I say (as we rattle over a cattle grid
and then squelch across a disinfectant mat,
not the first this morning that we've met)
a falling icicle caused the death
of a man who was walking underneath,
pole-axed as he sauntered with his wife,
right through his fur hat of sleek grey wolf,

the sharp tip with its glossy shine
sticking through his badly shaven chin.
In Leningrad you couldn't buy a blade
you'd get a decent shave from and not bleed.

An ice-bolt from malicious gods
could chill the skull and slice the vocal chords
of this Geordie smoker here, under threat,
getting quick drags of smoke into his throat,
banished the bank so many times a day
increasing the odds that maybe he will die,
this ostracized, cold, street-drag Damocles
under the half-thawed bank roof icicles.
The frozen, furtive smoker in shirt sleeves
under icicle-hung gutterings and eves
puffs fast on his cupped fag and quickly stubs
half out among the scattered kerbside tabs.

I enter Dobson's elegant colonnade,
its Railway Age proportions just renewed,
aware of risk and how a roof-slate slid,
only two days ago, a heavy slate,
off my front roof and cut the garden seat
where normally on warm days I'd've sat
and almost did that first bright day of March
when the sun woke up a solitary midge.
If the temperature had been two more degrees
I might have sat there and not cut my grass
so that the tile that weeks of gale winds loosed
missed me by metres and my skull's unsliced.

Yesterday ten passengers on this route died
which makes today's predictably subdued
like me, who's thinking did fate choose to spare
me from slate, and collision, as a kind of spur,
to go on doing what I do, that's look and write
as I've done since the sixties on this route?

I remember all the great books that I've read
I'd never 've started if I'd gone by road,
the poems, like this one, that I've written
some passable, and published, most though rotten.
I used to know the landmarks on this route
the industries of Britain left and right.
Once I'd know exactly where we were
from the shapes of spoil heaps and from winding gear
spinning their spokes and winching down a shift
miles deep into this sealed and filled-in shaft
and which bits of field you'd see a score
of rabbits in the passing train would scare,
which Yorkshire coal-dust-laquered black lagoon
had crested grebes on once but now long gone,
but once my own slack-blackened Hippocrene,
though the Pegasus would be more like that crane,
raising a replica of this coach, ripped and crushed
when yesterday's Newcastle–King's Cross crashed,
I see from a jerkily slow, jinxed British train
through snow, cremation smoke-clouds, quarantine.

If you still could get them open then I'd throw
these pages I've been scribbling, 1–2–3,

out of the window. All I've done so far
of *Cremation Eclogue* floats towards the fire,
where choking piles of stiff-legged Friesians blaze,
their piebald blending, poem into place.

WW

He wanders lonely as a cloud
to watch the cattle being culled.

I see the well-soled boot
of William's ghost on walkabout

dent the disinfectant mat.
He was declaiming when we met,

and all at once his eyes beheld
dead sheep bleeding in the field,

no stirring but wind-ruffled fleece
and rats and crows and worms and lice.

And the bard's iambic burst by coughs
caused by smoking cows and calves.

The victims in these MAFF culls
outnumbering the daffodils;

a JCB 's their mass-grave hearse
now rendered into smoke and verse.

Queueing for Charon

Cretans still can't stand 'the Krauts'
but don't turn them away,
gaga ex-Nazis, lager louts,
cramming Crete on holiday.
Fifty odd years of so-called peace
fill beaches with old foes.
Northern Europe flocks to Greece
to warm its frozen toes.
And my old carcass likes these coasts,
archaeology and joy,
but even in Greek sun the ghosts
come back to haunt the boy.
Underneath the skin that's tanned
these Krauts are frail and ill
but once they served the Fatherland
with more than time to kill.
This museum that they shuffle round
groggy from too much sun
has finds out of the Cretan ground
once trampled by the Hun.
Of an age to have yelled *Zieg Heils*,
worn jackboots, marched like geese,

they stagger round with vacant smiles
smeared with anti-UV grease.
A few years younger I'd only seen
Belsen on newsreels but the sight
I saw at eight on that big screen
fell on me like a blight.
It clouded all my childish fun.
My voice, before it got its bass,
squeaked against the humbled Hun
and murderous Master Race.
Younger than these Krauts on Crete
my old Hun-hatred flares.
They've come in to escape the heat
and dodder up the stairs.

These dodderers I demonize
aren't garbed in SS Might
but kit that bares their flabby thighs
and blistered cellulite.
An hour to kill till their lamb stew
then I can be left alone
to keep my promised rendezvous
with a laureate of bone.

2

A dolphin dominates the room
caught at the zenith of its arc
leaping inside an ancient tomb
from mortality's deep dark.

Once the painting had been done
it was hidden from the light
sealed with a lid that weighed a ton
and seamlessly sun-tight.
Do dolphins soar out of the deep
and, soaring, seem to pack
all joy there is into the leap
because they're going back?
I'd sooner see them live at sea
but this corpse's private view
shows the surface of mortality
their leaps keep breaking through.
The Germans think the dolphin's *schön*;
more comfort than the coffin quilt
cushioning them when it's their turn
to attempt a leap from guilt.
I saw a dolphin diver/flyer
from a ferry Lesbos bound
to where the floating head and lyre
of Orpheus ran aground.
And here's a skull with golden wreath
a sort of Orpheus but
songless for ever and his teeth
clamped permanently shut.
One jovial elder cracks a joke
that's meant to keep at bay
the thought that even *Herrenvolk*
end up as skulls one day.
It makes the old girls all guffaw,
but their laughter quickly dies

faced with the skull I stand before
whose sockets hold my eyes.
The Germans crowd me at the case
where the poet's skull's displayed.
It's fleshed by my reflected face
and when I leave reflayed.
The Gerriatrics quieten down
at the case where I am now,
a poet's skull with laurel crown
still on its bony brow.
What strikes me dumb is that I spy
the obol put inside his cheek
to pay his fare 's still there, but why?
Did the ferry bar this Greek?
Why the coin still with the skull?
Was it, as in these old folks' day,
that Charon's stiff-skiff was chock full
and the bard was turned away?
And turned away because art fails
when violence is rife
and doesn't help to tip the scales
towards the claims of life?
Are hearts touched by your great gifts
or softened just a jot?
Since I'm working double shifts
they're obviously not!
If any poems or piddling odes
can be shown (a monstrous if)
ever to have lightened my huge loads
I'll scull you in my skiff.

Charon said: *'Piss off, I'm full!*
At least to poets I am.'
That's why the obol's with the skull
all bards get told to scram.

And poets' obols are still leaning
against their fleshless jaw
because they failed to give a meaning
to all those ghosts of War.
I think for poets the moral 's
when they reach those Styx bank queues
they should ditch their golden laurels
and stand behind the queueing Jews
until the last one's safely crossed,
then poets might have their say.
Poetry since the Holocaust
's a Stygian stowaway.

3

Charon can't work any quicker
to clear the endless line
and the rear is getting thicker
with new blood from Palestine.
The bards are crowding on the banks
of this slithery nearer shore
with zlotys, kroner, pennies, francs
tucked inside their jaw,
and all of them doomed to repeat,
whatever tongue they speak,

the stutters of the skull of Crete
choking on his Greek.
The bards hope Charon won't capsize
with loads who 've lost their tongue
for what these Germans' shaded eyes
looked on when they were young,
these burned who leave to board their bus,
the red bus that reads Bonn,
making a gentle, gallant fuss
of sleeveless ladies they help on.
So the dumb poet with the wreath of gold
has he taught them any lesson?
Live every moment when you're old?
The bus moves. Next stop: *Essen!*
They'll leave the island in a week
and take the ferry back from Crete
with peppermints inside their cheek
to keep their short breath sweet.
From the ferry rail they scan the waves
and keep their weak eyes peeled
for dolphins that can leap from graves
before their lids are sealed.

über al

(Uns hat der winter geschadet über al . . .)

Winter 's done his worst all round,
leafless trees, and lifeless ground,
silence where birdsong used to sound.
I want summer back with girls at play
and birds that sing at break of day.

Till the birds bring back their song
I'd like to sleep all Winter long
while his stranglehold 's still strong.
But once May weakens Winter's powers
from this frostbound ground I'll pick you flowers.

(Walther von der Vogelweide, 1170–1230)

A Question of Sentences

(*Nuremburg, 1946*)

One Nazi 's tongue-tied, and one's tongue 's loose.
Speer lives to see his fluent *Memoirs* toasted.
One gets twenty years, and one the noose.
Sauckel's *Life* could only have been ghosted.

Speer enunciates, and Sauckel mutters.
Speer looks them in the eye. His *Deutsch* is *Hoch* –

Sauckel's heels go click! The whole man stutters,
strung up, a lifetime's words he never spoke.

Eggshells

One year in Washington DC
a girl I got to know
said she came from Germany.
She looked quite like Bardot.

And her first name was Brigitte
(rhymes with bitter not with sweet)
and though things turned out bitter
we met for walks, for drinks, to eat.

In a little while she let me see
her total tan, breasts, belly, legs.
And that Easter Sunday in DC
she brought me Easter eggs.

She'd painted all the eggs by hand
with folk-style whorls and flowers
in the manner of her fatherland.
It took her hours and hours.

Daddy took my hand to guide
the brush's gleaming tip
and held it firm when fuss outside
might make me smudge or slip . . .

I stuck out my tongue like this
(I knew that tongue quite well)
to master all that artifice
we both lavished on the shell.

The eggs in an ashtray by my bed
with their gay patterns made me glad
but, on our next date, Brigitte said
I should know more about her Dad.

Before you get too fond of me
I've got something to confess,
she said that April in DC
in her Yves St Laurent dress.

If her face said it was bad,
when the words came it was worse.
My Washington bedfellow's dad,
she said, was Rudolf Hoess.

Though I hugged her when we said goodbye
I couldn't face her after that.
Though I still admired the artistry
I squashed the frail eggs flat.

In Poland I saw where she was shown
to make yellow out of onion peel
and they'd decorate the eggs he'd blown,
the Kommandant, with cochineal.

Delicate execution learned,
helped by sticking out her tongue,
where millions were gassed and burned
and egg-dyeing Dad was hung.

No doubt she still tops up the tan
on bronzed belly, breasts and legs,
and dreams one day she'll find a man
who won't smash her Easter eggs.

The Grilling

I'd just walked up and down Vesuvio
as Goethe did two centuries ago.
At the bottom with a bottle of white wine
I heard the great poet talking to Tischbein:

Vesuvio puffing smoke out not far off
flavours this fine vino that we quaff.
That force that belches forth its molten mass
has poured this tinkling gold in my raised glass.
Devastation, Tischbein, ancient waste
gives this Vesuvial vintage its fine taste.
While we're drinking let's remember hope 's
what goes with hoe in hand to smoking slopes,
ploughs blistering cinders into ashy fields
knowing the fine vines cooled lava yields.
Before the hoers came and earth showed green
singed Satyrs would be first back on the scene,
as before spectators' tears have time to dry
the Satyrs enter with their cock-tips high.
After the mask, with always opened eyes
seeing the worst, the phallus of gross size.
When lust for life is bankrupt, head and heart
get bridging loans from that exuberant part.

I think of the Satyrs dancing on the coals
and celebrating life with blistered soles,
or, if seen as half-horse, hooves, not feet,
gelatinous from jigging on that heat,
and they dance more featly, fleeter, faster
because their dancefloor 's on the site of a disaster.
Does their acrobatic goat/horse/man gavotte
come from the ground they jig on being hot?
All I'm suggesting is we might enquire
if the dancing is dependant on the fire.
Tragedies, extinctions and the night
trodden by dancing into draughts of light.
The world's unjust to Satyrs. They enact
a valetudinous Walpurgisnacht.

(I'm pretending not to notice, but I see
Tischbein, all this while, 's been sketching me!)
Goethe's in full flow. I see him glug
two great draughts of wine straight from the jug
I knew he liked to drink. His favourite wine
came from Würzburg's vineyards on the Main.
I felt like saying it's OK for you –
your cut-off point is 1832!
Between then and my own day
there've been far worst disasters than Pompeii . . .

Once he's glugged his wine I hear him say:

Martial, that poet of Priapus, remembers
love's green haunts beneath the glowing embers,

40

a dappling of grape pattern where sun shone
on slopes ash scoria now slither on.
It's this ash-strewn, bleak volcano, this
that Marcus Valerius Martialis
makes so vine-clad and beloved of Bacchus,
those oozing wine vats, madidos lacus,
and this, black as it looks today, the Satyrs
dedicated to Dionysian matters.
I've never been particularly partial
to the rather puerile epigrams of Martial,
but his poem, particularly the last line,
rather tolls the knell of the divine.
More wine! More figs! And while I pour
read me Epigrams IV.xliv.
Thank God for real figs, not those charred
Pompeian relics carbonized and hard.

Tischbein looks it up, and line by line
reads it for Goethe's benefit. And mine:

Hic est pampineis viridis modo Vesuvius umbris
    presserat hic madidos nobilis uva lacus
haec iuga, quam Nysae colles plus Bacchus amavit;
    hoc nuper Satyri monte dedere choros;
haec Veneris sedes, Lacedaemone gratior illi;
    hic locus Herculeo numine clarus erat.
cuncta iacent flammis et tristi mersa favilla
    nec superi vollent hoc licuisse sibi.

They improvised translations and sipped wine.
Here's Thomas May's then Addison's then mine:

Vesuvius, shaded once with greenest vines
Where pressed grapes did yield the noblest wines;
Which hill far more than Nysa Bacchus lov'd,
Where satyrs once in mirthful dances mov'd,
Where Venus dwelt, and better lov'd the place
Than Sparta where Alcides temple was,
Is now burnt downe, rak'd up in ashes sad.
The gods are grill'd that such great power they had.

(Thomas May 1595–1650)

(*grill* as in to grieve to hurt, give pain,
grill as in 'The grones of sir Gawayne
does my heart grille'. But *grill* as well has heat
and whatever gods there were have blistered feet.)

'Vesuvius cover'd with the fruitful vine,
Here flourish'd once, and ran with floods of wine:
Here Bacchus oft to the cool shades retired,
And his own native Nysa less admired:
Oft to the mountain's airy tops advanced,
The frisking Satyrs on the summits danced:
Alcides here, here Venus, graced the shore,
Nor loved her favourite Lacedaemon more.
Now piles of ashes, spreading all around
In undistinguish'd heaps, deform the ground:
The gods themselves the ruin'd seats bemoan,
And blame the mischiefs that themselves have done.'

(Joseph Addison 1672–1719)

42

Vesuvius, green yesterday with shady vine,
*   where the crushed grape gushed vast vats of wine,*
ridges, Bacchus loved and put before
*   his birthplace Nysa, Venus favoured more*
than Lacedaemon, and where Satyrs stomped
*   till now, and Herculaneum, all swamped,*
engulfed by cinders in a flood of fire:

power like this not even gods desire.

Martial IV.44

(Tony Harrison 1937–   )

Goethe dashed his own off, and his wine
in which he tasted AD 79,
then spoke to my portraitist Tischbein:

The gods are grilled to have such dreadful powers.
But what gods' hands let go of ends in ours.
What Martial's gods say no to, Man says yes;
his cold palm weighs the orb of Nothingness.
Gods refuse the powers and late Man weighs
like a regent the recentest of days.
Drink!
*   There is no danger of the thing erupting?*

Excuse me, *Meine Herren,* excuse my interrupting . . .
I've just been listening to your conversation
about wine tasting of old devastation.
Vesuvio, vine-enricher and crop killer
spouting fatal/fertile hot *favilla.*

In Santorini vines from cliffs of clinker
give, even to the life-affirming drinker,
an old extinction in its strange bouquet
the Knossos catastrophe haunts that wine today.
Pompeian figs turned carbon in their bowl
can only, if you'd crunch them, taste of coal
figs from the cinders now can still taste sweet
but the wine still has the tang of rubbled Crete.
How does the *vino* here compare to wine
you're said to have drunk so much of from the Main?
Not under the volcano the vines there
but in '45 our fire rained from the air.
Not volcanic wine but since we bombed it flat
disaster goes with grapes into the vat.
If you drank those Main wines now you'd taste
Würzburg and its vintages laid waste,
Würzburg where you bought 'goat's scrota' from
was levelled by the British *Fire Bomb*,
bodies in the poses of Pompeii
9000 filled the rubbled streets next day.

(Wine in glass *Bocksbeuteln* (goats' scrota)
from Würzurg was the *Lieblingstrank* of Goethe.)
and all the glass goat's scrota popped
and fused together when the bombs were dropped.
From that molten mass of glass like boiling glue
Riesling steam clouds rose into the blue.
Does that *Stein Wein*, you guzzled taste the same
after the vineyards passed through fire-storm flame?

Würzburg vintners always quote the line
your *gewohnter Lieblingstrank Frankischer Wein*
your, at least reputed, yearly quota
of *sehr gut* gluggable 'goats' scrota'
was 900 litres – well, I suppose
colleagues in Weimar quaffed some of those.

Entschuldigung, Herr Goethe, Herr Tischbein,
I didn't want to spoil lunch with my story.
Let me at least replenish your white wine:

Cameriere, Vesuvio bianco per le signori!

Signori? Questi? Dove? you OK?
Sit there, talk to self all bloody day.

But Tischbein had torn his sketch out of his book
me, half finished with a haunted look.
Behind me smudged with spilled Vesuvial wine
a cloud from the crater shaped like Pliny's pine.
I picked it up but in one blinding flash
it erupted into flame and turned to ash.
On one frail flake the outline of an eye
went floating on the heat into the sky.

Reading the Rolls: An Arse-Verse

[note: arse-verse: West Yorkshire: a spell on a house to ward off fire. *ars* > *ardere* Lat; burn, as in *arson*.]

> *quin etiam passim nostris in versibus ipsis*
> *multa elementa vides multis communia verbis,*
> *cum tamen inter se versus ac verba necessest*
> *confiteare et re et sonitu distare sonanti.*
> *tantum elementa queunt permutato ordine solo.*

(Lucretius, *De Rerum Natura*, 1.823–827)

I

The Pythia on her rock seat
inhaling rot learned to recite
before Homer's age the very first
hexameters a human voiced.
Full of reek, dead dragon slouch,
the reptile on its rocky ledge,
the putrid serpent, was the true
inspirer of pure poetry.

With thoughts like these I'd reconcile
those years of writing with the smell

of leaking gas and fantasized
of serpents when the gas-fire hissed.
It helped me concentrate, the hiss
like that of the clobbered Pythoness
Apollo clubbed to one long bruise,
a serpent pelt the champion's prize,
clobbered so Apollo could
be Delphi's one presiding god.
He clubbed his way to serpent's lair
then swapped flesh-coated club for lyre,
but still rank bits of snake-gut fly
when the god's in full lyre-maestro flow.
The Muse who did his manicure
forgot to clean his nails of gore.
So when Apollo plucks the strings
pure music comes with serpent stinks.

Through over thirty years of writing
miasma from the monster's rotting,
seeping through pine and carpet wool,
was the inspiration I'd inhale.
I've tolerated that vague whiff
but now they've turned my gas taps off . . .
rank reptile guts, bad gas escapes
from my dodgy cracked lead pipes.
Not old gas now, thank God! – CO 's
what the suicidal mostly chose
(and once when I tried to choose which
gas came joint top with Tyne Bridge).
It's long been North Sea I hear hiss

like the sleeping Delphi Pythoness
whose crusted viscera and bones
they've just dumped in my rubbish bins.
with all my fires though I pleaded –

You're lucky none of 'em exploded.

Commotion over such a smell
I can recall when very small.
There's summat snuffed it under t'floor
granpa said *Get Freddy Flea.*
Fred, for fifty years, had toured
with his flea circus. Now retired
he'd get called in to help pinpoint
where rats had died and earn a pint.
Fred's kennel of winged tracker dogs
were bluebottles in a *Lifeboat* box.
Fred let them out, that's all he did
to find out where the rat had died.
They buzzed and settled. Once Fred knew
the spot where all his trackers flew
he raised a floorboard to reveal a
rotting rat *voila, voila!*
Fred's trackers got their own reward.
My first lesson as the rat's devoured
how what's alive thrives on what's not.
Then Fred caught them in a little net
and pushed their bright blue faience backs
back into the *Lifeboat* box.

II

I'm aware today the earliest verse
I ever mumbled wiped my arse,
enjoyed for what they were, not judged,
torn off the roll, and used, and flushed.
No poems now on toilet paper
(imagine slim flat-packs from Faber,
but not the sort of verse one reads
and harder on the haemorrhoids!).
But then when I was just gone four
and in the second year of war,
I unrolled poems to recite
precarious on the toilet seat,
some bright quatrain not epic saga
to be consigned to the cloaca.
Those moments I communed with metre
set me on course to be a writer.
From those rough sheets I learned to read
verses in the smell of rot,
dumped dactyl, and turd-smeared trochee
primed the prosodics of decay.

I can't recite the sort of ditty
I remember reading in the netty.
I remember rhythms not the words
that went with war-time infant turds,
but I do remember one
that pitched poetics at the Hun,

the raving loo-roll Hitler
bulls-eyed by the childish piddler.
The flush-churned *Führer* screams
and below him in red writhing rhymes:

Hitler now screams with impatience
Our good health is proving a strain
May he and his Axis relations
Soon find themselves right down the drain . . .

Lord Chesterfield's advice
to his son was Latin verse,
not lengthy epics like Lucretius
dangerous and irreligious,
but shorter poems like Horace *Odes*
construed while extruding turds,
a page per shit for the beginner
before consigned to Cloacina.
Lise, Ragueneau,
the baker's wife in *Cyrano*
wrapped brioche and quiche and tart
in poems by the baker/bard.
Poor old Heine dreamed his *Lieder*
made baccy wrap or fire lighter.
Two centuries ago
Drury Lane made storms of snow
from the shredded pages of the plays
of poets who had failed to please.
Shred me for snow, I'd like these pages
drifting down while Lear rages.

Or feel free in need to use these verses,
if not too rough, to wipe your arses.

[but there is no perforation here
continue sitting do not tear . . .]

III

[If you've not yet wiped your arse
it's either 1. because my verse,
more captivating than reputed,
grips you, or 2. you're constipated!]

A Philodemus poem's apt:
[could be read three times while you crapped]
life's a papyrus being ripped
column by column as it's read
and no one ever can re-read.
Apter though, I think, by far
is this charred roll as metaphor.
Poetry and the human soul.
A carbonized papyrus scroll
taking months to read an inch
unwound on the rack-cum-winch
contraption of Piaggio
who daily sketched Vesuvio
over two centuries ago.
Tightening the silk rack's screw
black syllables slide into view.
Each day another millimetre

made visible to that rare reader
whose eye could con such text and crack
the secrets of black script on black.
What's this illegible black writing
on carbonized papyrus hiding?
Tilting it this way and then that
reveals a radiant alphabet.
The black on black is not a blank.
Light flashes from the lamp-soot ink,
words in iridescent lustre
like the nacre of the oyster,
a lustre like black mackerel scales
or like the peacock coal of Wales.
What iridesces is philosophy
that aims to free the mind from fear
and put the old gods out to grass
and live life in the moment's grace.
The philosopher is infamous
as the poet Philodemus
Cicero called a Greekling creep
whose fawning poetry was crap,
who flattered Piso, one of Rome's
known layabouts, in tacky rhymes.
He brown-nosed Piso and got lodged
and looked on while his patron leched,
luxuriated, lounged and lauded
the Epicurus he diluted
especially for Piso's taste:
all life boiled down to getting pissed,
the *diem carpe*d in good booze

(Chian, of course!), eels, turbot; boys.
Though it's claimed that Xanthippe,
his wife, kept Philodemus happy,
it's Flora's blazoned boobs and arse
that bob up often in his verse
addressed and undressed with the O's
Epicureans always use.
O, poetry's fundamental core,
chrysanthemums in Zen haiku.
To begin with put down eight
like a beauty queen parade.
ω ω ω ω ω ω ω ω
8 omegas all in a row,
all loose and ready to apply
wherever lust or wonder blow.
Though omega stands for what's last,
in his poems of love and lust
you'll see Philodemus add
that letter of the alphabet
as *blason anatomique*,
an O or exclamation mark
before or after all the bits
a sensual lover celebrates:
ω γλουτων, ω κτενος, ω λαγονων.
O plus the lingered-over noun
from cunt with little comb-like fringe
to kissing (definitely French!)
foot, shoulders, breasts, all get
the last letter of the alphabet –
ω ω ω ω

Omegas are O's not Ah's
Its sound is O, its shape an arse,
a 42nd St chorine's,
a 50s swimsuit beauty queen's.
John Donne's 'O my America!'
works like the Greek poet's omega,
Flora's shoulders! breasts! neck! thighs!
to add O to or apostrophize,
apostrophizing buttocks, cunt
and how she moves them: *'If she can't*
recite a Sapphic ode OK!
So she's called Flora I don't care!
her name is Flora from the sticks
she's a real star when she fucks.'

This is philosphy reduced
to loving flesh that turns to dust
entropy's attractive butt
before the O-hailed flesh or fruit,
as though the grasped IS IS IS IS
is balanced on a precipice.
Colours intensify, not fade
against annihilating void.
But all it needs to do that O
as we *carpe diem* is to grow
and we'll go straight into its maw.
Once it gets out of control
it swallows all we're praising whole.
The O we use to mark our joy
needs but to widen to destroy,

to suck fellators and their O's
down the void's vast vacuum hose.

Life is atoms and the void
of which we shouldn't be afraid,
says Titus Lucretius Carus,
poet/follower of Epicurus,
in scrolls still buried from the doom
that fell on Herculaneum.
Carbonized in 79
their iridescence now may drown.
Still interred unlike the Greek
papyri we've begun to crack,
packed *capsae* of papyri fated
to be flooded if unexcavated.
Maybe the *De Rerum Natura*
made accessibly much clearer
on how the chemistry that recombines
the consonants of verbs and nouns
is like the void where atoms dance,
alliteration, assonance,
the voiced and voiceless counterparts
used in *cynghanedd* by Welsh bards,
p/b k/g s/z t/d
pairs in disparate unity
which makes the listener or reader
through a great O-sweeping radar
aware of bright life *and* life's undertow
of chaos tugging from below.
In a charred Lucretius each new clue

needs lacunae and the black to glow.
And from each alphabetic spark
work out the letters left in dark
Bright *g* . . . bright *d* . . . or *n* . . . bright *o*
with void around brings vertigo,
but iridescences deciphered claim
all radiance enhanced by gloom,
and knowing this the soul is freed
from what before made it afraid.

The soul goes with cloacal matters
as much as tragedy with satyrs,
so, If you're still sitting on the loo
where your ω fits in an O,
peruse these prosodics from my pen,
then use, and flush them down the pan.

[Though perhaps for average shits
I've given you too many sheets.]

POCKET PENGUINS

36. **Muriel Spark** The Snobs
37. **Steven Pinker** Hotheads
38. **Tony Harrison** Under the Clock
39. **John Updike** Three Trips
40. **Will Self** Design Faults in the Volvo 760 Turbo
41. **H. G. Wells** The Country of the Blind
42. **Noam Chomsky** Doctrines and Visions
43. **Jamie Oliver** Something for the Weekend
44. **Virginia Woolf** Street Haunting
45. **Zadie Smith** Martha and Hanwell
46. **John Mortimer** The Scales of Justice
47. **F. Scott Fitzgerald** The Diamond as Big as the Ritz
48. **Roger McGough** The State of Poetry
49. **Ian Kershaw** Death in the Bunker
50. **Gabriel García Márquez** Seventeen Poisoned Englishmen
51. **Steven Runciman** The Assault on Jerusalem
52. **Sue Townsend** The Queen in Hell Close
53. **Primo Levi** Iron Potassium Nickel
54. **Alistair Cooke** Letters from Four Seasons
55. **William Boyd** Protobiography
56. **Robert Graves** Caligula
57. **Melissa Bank** The Worst Thing a Suburban Girl Could Imagine
58. **Truman Capote** My Side of the Matter
59. **David Lodge** Scenes of Academic Life
60. **Anton Chekhov** The Kiss
61. **Claire Tomalin** Young Bysshe
62. **David Cannadine** The Aristocratic Adventurer
63. **P. G. Wodehouse** Jeeves and the Impending Doom
64. **Franz Kafka** The Great Wall of China
65. **Dave Eggers** Short Short Stories
66. **Evelyn Waugh** The Coronation of Haile Selassie
67. **Pat Barker** War Talk
68. **Jonathan Coe** 9th & 13th
69. **John Steinbeck** Murder
70. **Alain de Botton** On Seeing and Noticing